Rebuilding Your Credit

Work the system, improve your credit score, sleep well

By

Neacel Marcas

Rebuilding Your Credit

Copyright © 2017

All rights reserved. This book or any portion thereof may not be reproduced or used in any manner whatsoever without the express written permission of the publisher except for the use of brief quotations in a book review.

ISBN: 9781520260426

Warning and Disclaimer

Every effort has been made to make this book as accurate as possible. However, no warranty or fitness is implied. The information provided is on an "as-is" basis. The author and the publisher shall have no liability or responsibility to any person or entity with respect to any loss or damages that arise from the information in this book.

Publisher Contact

Skinny Bottle Publishing

books@skinnybottle.com

Introduction 1

Understanding Your Credit Score 3

    What is a Bad Credit Score? 3

    What is the Average Score? 4

    What is a Good Score? 4

    What is an Excellent Score? 4

    Is your Fico Score Fixed? 5

Your Credit Report 6

    Getting Your Credit Report 7

    Now Let's Look at That Report 7

    What Type of Credit do you Have? 8

    Your Payment History 8

    How Much Debt You Might Get Into 9

    How Many Accounts You Have 10

    How Much do you Actually Owe? 10

What to Check on Your Report 12

    Check the Report for Errors 12

    Is the Report Up to Date? 13

    Are There any Arrears or Outstanding Debts? 14

Start Repairing Your Credit 16

    Pay Your Bills on Time 16

    Stop Maxing out Your Credit 17

    Time Your Withdrawals Carefully 18

    Pay More than the Monthly Minimum 19

    Pay Down Your Debt 20

    Manage Your Credit Limits 21

Start Working the System 22

    You Need Some Credit 22

    Getting a Secured Credit Card 23

    Get Installment Finance 24

    Limit Credit Applications 25

    Be Consistent and Persevere 26

    The Last Step 26

Conclusion 28

Introduction

For a lot of people, mistakes made early on when managing their credit come back to haunt them later in life, even when they are trying to be more fiscally responsible. Having bad credit can seem like a nightmare that you simply cannot wake up from and when you have gotten yourself back on your feet, you might be completely credit-shy.

You might not even feel that it is necessary to bother about your credit rating anymore – after all, what else could it possibly affect, right? Wrong, your credit rating affects more than just your ability to get finance.

Getting finance when you have bad credit becomes difficult at best. Even when the finance company will offer you a loan, the rate charged can be prohibitively expensive. This can put your dream of owning your own home or qualifying for emergency finance when you need it far out of reach.

Fortunately, though, some people can get by without credit – it takes some careful planning but it can be done. Unfortunately, the bad credit report may be holding you back in terms of your career and getting a better job as well. It is standard operating practice for potential employers to run a credit check on you before employing you and bad credit may interfere with your chances of being hired.

Life is also generally more expensive when you have bad credit – think I am talking nonsense? Did you know that your insurance premium is, in part, calculated taking your credit rating into account? The premium that you pay is a reflection of what risk the company believes that you pose for the company – and your credit rating plays a part of this. (If you have a bad credit record, you might end up missing payments on your policy and this can be a big problem for insurance companies, especially if you have already claimed.)

In addition, those credit facilities that you do still have will wind up costing your more because of your bad credit rating – unless your interest rate is fixed, the companies do regular reviews of your credit rating to determine what interest rate you are paying and, even if you pay your account on time each month, a bad credit rating will have an impact.

In terms of all of this, therefore, it makes sense to take steps to repair your credit, as soon as you can. The good news – there are simple steps that you can take, starting today to improve your rating. If you follow these steps faithfully, you will be able to improve your credit score over time.

The bad news – it will not happen overnight. As I said before, this is a process. Your credit history looks at your average behavior, with special weighting being placed on the last 6 months. Paying your accounts on time this month will help but it will not be enough to repair a previously bad score. Only consistency will pay the greatest dividends.

In this book, I am going to focus on the U.S. FICO system but the tips can be applied to other countries as well.

Understanding Your Credit Score

In this chapter, we will go through some basics so that you understand what lies at the core of your credit report, your credit score, and how it affects you. Your credit score can be seen as an amalgamation of all of your credit history – you get points for doing things right, like paying your bills on time, and have points deducted when you do things wrong, like paying less than the minimum installment.

In this instance, I will go through the FICO scoring system we use in the U.S. so that you can see exactly what constitutes a good score and bad one.

What is a Bad Credit Score?

In this case, you want the highest score possible. If your score is 619 or less, you are considered a bad credit risk and are unlikely to be able to access any form of financing. A score this low indicates someone that has arrears in terms of their bills is a constant bad payer or maybe even someone with debt that is in collection.

What is the Average Score?

The average American has a score of around 692 and this is considered a fair score.

If you score is between 620 and 699, you are considered a fair risk and, while you may be able to get financing, you are going to have to pay for that privilege. Scores that fall within this range are still considered low and higher risk when it comes to lending.

What is a Good Score?

If you have a fico score of between 700 and 749, you have a good rating.

If you fall into this category, you will find it easier to get credit as this score generally indicates that you are a responsible lender and are reasonably good at keeping your accounts up to date. This indicates that you never allow your bills to become more than 30 days overdue.

What may surprise you is that you still won't have access to the very best interest rates that the company has to offer. These are reserved for those with excellent credit.

What is an Excellent Score?

To fall into this category, you need to have a credit rating of 750 – 850. If you do fall in this category, you have proven that you manage your debt responsibly, always pay on time and seldom, if ever, max out your cards. This is what most credit providers would classify as the perfect borrower and the rates that are offered will reflect that.

It is the classic conundrum – you can really only get a great deal on credit if you can prove that you do not need credit.

Is your Fico Score Fixed?

Fortunately, if you have a bad credit rating, your FICO score is not some immutable number – you can actually work at improving it by modifying your actions over time. As long as you are consistent in your attempts, you will be able to get your FICO score to increase.

The truth is that it is simple to work the system so that your score improves. It can be something as simple as waiting a week or so after paying your credit card before using it again, or even just bumping up the amount you pay every month.

And you can monitor the progress so you can see what is working and what is not. What is also great is that whilst these steps may not drastically improve your FICO score immediately, the companies who monitor these things will be able to see that your overall behavior in terms of your debt has changed – they will see that you are becoming a more responsible borrower and that you are better able to manage the debt that you have. This can be a big positive for you.

Your Credit Report

Want to know what the first step is? It is simple, find out where you stand now. I have counselled a lot of people with bad credit – I even used to have bad credit myself so I know how scary this step can be.

After all, it is one thing to know at the back of your mind that you have a bad credit score but it is quite another to actually confront that score in black and white on the page. This is scary – it basically means that you can no longer deny how bad things actually are.

If, however, you can bring yourself to do it anyway, you are actually freeing yourself from a lot of worries in the future – you might even find out that things are not as bad as you thought. You really do not have much of a choice – you need to see your report to see how to go about fixing it.

Getting Your Credit Report

It is not that hard to lay hands on your credit report – in fact, you simply have to apply to the credit bureaus – you are entitled to one free credit report annually.

It is important to apply for your report from each of the three major credit bureaus – Experian, Transunion, and Equifax as the reports can vary from one to the next. Basically, it depends on which unions your credit providers subscribe to. (The credit bureaus basically just amalgamate the information received from the various credit providers in order to generate your payment profile and FICO score.)

If you do not want to apply to each individual site, there are websites that will do this for you – all you will need to do is to provide the relevant information and they will submit the requests to the credit bureaus on your behalf.

Now Let's Look at That Report

Now that you have your report in front of you, you need to start looking at it objectively – pretend that it is a stranger's report and that they have asked you to lend them money. You need to look at the report as if you were the lender, not the borrower and there will be a few things that you need to consider. Let's go through these individually.

What Type of Credit do you Have?

Credit is credit, right? Well, and I have to admit that this was something that surprised me when I learned about it, no – the type of credit that you utilize is used as an indicator of whether you are a responsible lender or not.

Now, in general, credit can be divided up into two broad categories – revolving credit and installment credit. Revolving credit, like the kind that you get with a credit card, is a more open-ended arrangement – as long as you are managing it properly and are paying as you should, you will still have access to the full credit limit. In essence, this means that you could use all the funds, less fees, and interest, that you pay into the card. You could, potentially, never pay off this debt.

An installment credit agreement is not open-ended at all. You will choose the term that you wish to repay your debt at and you will need to make those monthly payments as agreed. As the term of the loan progresses, the balance of the debt is reduced and, normally, you will not be allowed to draw that money out again.

Which do you think is considered riskier when it comes to new potential lenders?

Your Payment History

You remember when you thought that you could just slide on the last month's payment, or you just missed it by a couple of days? All that information is recorded on your payment history. And, even if you pay your accounts as little as one day late every month, you will be listed as a slow payer.

This is something that people just don't often realize – the importance of paying your bills on time every month. Your payment history is one of the things that a potential creditor will look at carefully because past behavior is the best predictor of future behavior. If you have a long string of late payments, that gives the impression that you are unable to afford your current debt or that you are irresponsible when it comes to paying bills – either way, it is a bad reflection on you as a borrower.

And it is good to remember that whilst the FICO score only takes the latest 6 months into account, your full payment history for each account is still listed. So that means that you need to be consistent in your efforts and keep up the new good behavior as anyone viewing your credit report will be able to see the full payment history.

How Much Debt You Might Get Into

This is another thing that people seldom realize makes a difference. Let us say that you are a responsible borrower and never max out your cards – what are your credit limits? A potential creditor will need to look at the overall amount of debt that you might be able to access – maybe today you haven't used your store card limit but there is nothing stopping you from doing so at a later stage.

If you went and spent just an extra $500 on 4 of your cards, your debt could, for example, have increased by $2000 in an instant and your whole repayment profile would have changed as well.

How Many Accounts You Have

The fact is that credit is a fickle mistress – you have to have some accounts that you pay in order to prove that you are credit worthy. Once you have proved that you are credit worthy, it will seem as though everyone wants to offer you credit. The problem with having too many credit accounts from a creditor's point of view is not only that you have a higher potential exposure.

It can also be viewed as a sign that you are unable to manage your finances. Why do you have 3 credit cards and 5 store cards, if you are so good at managing your money?

How Much do you Actually Owe?

This is a big one, obviously but there are a couple of different things to consider under this heading.

First of all, how much is your overall exposure to debt and how does this affect your ability to repay it? Creditors want to see that you can not only manage the debt that you currently have but also that you can manage the debt that you are applying for.

Repayments for debt, excluding mortgage debt, should be, at most, 30% of your overall monthly salary – AFTER deductions. Your mortgage should not exceed 30% of your overall monthly salary AFTER deductions either.

More importantly for creditors, though, is how you utilize the credit that you do already have. It is in this area that most people actually come short when it comes to the difference between that great credit score and the good or fair one.

Think about it for a second, if your friend had maxed out all their cards and gotten loans all over the place and then still came over to you to come and get a loan, would you be happy to give it to them?

Constantly maxing out your credit limits, especially when these are revolving credit limits, is a strong indicator of one of two things – either you have more debt than you can handle and need to use credit to supplement your income or you are irresponsible when it comes to spending. If you want to fall into the excellent category in terms of your FICO score, you should not be using over 30% of your credit limits at any stage. (does not apply to mortgage limits)

What to Check on Your Report

Now that you have a better idea of what your credit standing is and now that you understand how a creditor would view the report, you can start taking the following steps to repair your credit.

I just want to emphasize here that consistency will be rewarded – this is not an easy process but the work will be worthwhile when you have a much better credit score.

Check the Report for Errors

The first thing to do is to check to see whether or not there are any mistakes on the report. Do you know about all the accounts and amounts on the report? Be sure that no one has fraudulently used your details to open accounts, that the amounts listed are correct and that they are amounts that pertain to you.

If you do find any errors here, you can apply to the credit bureau concerned to lodge a dispute. Legally speaking, they have 30 days in which to answer claims that have been submitted in writing and defend the information that they have listed.

You will need to complete a form provided by the company and explain why you believe that the information is erroneous. You will be expected to produce some documentary evidence in support of this.

If it is found that the listing was placed on your account in error, they are required by law to remove the said listing. The onus is on them to be able to prove that the information is verifiable and this works in your favor.

Is the Report Up to Date?

Perhaps you had a doctor's bill that you paid late and have a negative listing as a result. Even if you have since paid the bill, there is no obligation from the doctor's side to have the listing removed or even to mark that it has been paid in full. The listing will simply remain in place for 5-10 years if nothing is done about it.

Check the negative listings on your account and, where these have been paid in full, gather up your proofs of payment. Then contact the companies concerned and ask whether or not, seeing as you have paid the debt, they would consider removing the listing altogether. Some companies have policies in place that prevent them from removing the listing altogether but they do have an obligation to at least mark the debt as having been settled.

Approach the companies calmly and be polite – getting rude and demanding your "rights" is bound to get you nowhere fast. Try to get them on your side and be willing to submit proof of payment where necessary.

In the case of a judgement, things may become a little more complicated as the judgement is a matter of public record and should be removed by court order or left in place until it expires naturally.

If you like, you can go the route of applying for the details of the judgement – should any of these details be incorrect, let's say a middle initial is wrong or your name has been misspelled, you can apply to have the judgement invalidated.

Getting the judgement invalidated is the simplest route to go to have a judgement removed.

If all the details are valid, and you can provide proof that you have repaid the funds, you can apply to the courts to have the judgement rescinded or at least marked as paid.

Are There any Arrears or Outstanding Debts?

Check for arrears on your current bills and try to figure out a way to start paying off these arrears. Examine your budget for ways to cut back so that you can afford to repay the arrears. Set up a payment plan that you will be able to stick to every month and make sure that you can afford it.

From there, contact your creditors with your proposed payment plan and see whether or not there is anything that they can do to facilitate your catching up on the arrears amount. For this to work, you will need to pay the minimum monthly installment plus something on the arrears amount as well. Perhaps your creditor can help to refinance the arrears in some manner so that you seem to be up to date with your accounts again.

If you cannot afford to make extra payments to catch up the arrears, you still need to work out a payment plan that you can manage and then contact the creditor to see whether or not they will accept it. For this to work, the amount has to be reasonable for both of you – your creditors will be more willing to work with you if you approach them with a reasonable offer. Your proposed payment should at least cover the interest and still pay something off the capital amount monthly as well.

If, for example, you have a credit card debt of $2000, offering to pay $20 a month is not reasonable because it does not even cover the interest installment.

The bottom line is that if you want to repair your credit, your best way to do this is to get your arrears caught up as soon as possible. If you do have to have a payment plan put in place going forward, do make sure that you adhere to this plan properly as not doing so will also negatively impact your credit rating.

Start Repairing Your Credit

Right, now we are ready to start working on building a better credit profile for you going forward. Remember that it is the latest data that bears the strongest weight in the calculation of your credit score and so what you start doing from today can have an impact, even if you only start off slowly.

Pay Your Bills on Time

Once the arrears are settled, you need to ensure that you pay each and every single one of your bills when it is due, where possible, even paying early if you can.

Also, take into account the time it will take to process your payment when deciding when to pay your bills. If for example, you pay your bills by mailing a check, you need to ensure that there is enough time for the check to reach the company concerned and to be banked before your bill is due.

This is possibly the best way to demonstrate to potential creditors and existing ones that you are becoming more responsible when it comes to managing your credit and that you are managing your debt in a more responsible manner.

Paying your bills on time has an enormously positive impact on your credit rating. It is important to note that here I am not just referring to paying off credit agreements but also to paying off your other monthly bills like gas, cable, etc. Most companies that have ongoing agreements with their clients will report payment history to at least one of the credit bureaus.

Your aim must be to pay everything on time – paying any bill, no matter how small, late every month sends a strong message to a potential creditor – that you are either over-indebted or that you cannot manage your money. After all, let's say you keep paying a gas bill of $40 a month late – how can you be trusted with a loan or credit card installment that is two or three times the amount if you cannot handle a small bill like that?

Stop Maxing out Your Credit

At the height of my credit craziness, I had 11 credit cards, 7 store cards, 4 personal loans and a mortgage, totaling thousands of dollars. I actually got to a stage where I stopped opening my mail because I was scared to face reality.

Naturally, I tried to apply for another loan in order to help me out – I thought it was my only option – and I was horrified when it was declined due to over-indebtedness. I couldn't understand it – I was paying all my accounts on time and doing everything "right". Except that, I was maxing out my cards every single month. I would make a payment and then immediately draw the money out again, usually on the same day.

As a result, my credit rating dropped faster – if you are using the full credit limit available to you, you are showing the creditors that you are battling to manage the debt. Think about it for a second, someone who is comfortably off will not usually max out all their cards constantly, they do not need to.

Once your arrears have been caught up, and you are paying your bills on time every month, start looking at how you can reduce your balances on your credit accounts. Remember, for you to have an excellent score, you need to aim for a credit usage ratio of no more than 30% of your credit limit.

Start rethinking what you are buying on your accounts or credit cards.

Time Your Withdrawals Carefully

If you have no choice but to use the full credit limit every month, time your withdrawals more carefully. Leave at least two to three days between the time that you pay the card and the time that you withdraw the money so that your card is not constantly maxed out. This will also help you to save a little in terms of credit interest.

Another tip that works quite well is to pay your whole grocery allowance into your card and buy as and when necessary – while the allowance is still in your card, it is reducing your overall balance and doing you some good at the same time. (Only use the allowance, though, not the credit limit here.)

You can also try changing the date of payments of non-interest bearing accounts. Say, for example, that you get paid on the last day of every month and that your insurance payment goes through on the 1st of every month. Can you move the date to the 15th and store the money in an accessible credit card or your access mortgage bond from the date you got paid until just before the payment is due? If you have the self-discipline to make this work, you can save a lot in terms of interest and can also help to improve your credit score at the same time.

Pay More than the Monthly Minimum

Paying only the monthly minimum on your debt is a sign of a borrower who is either irresponsible or one who is over-indebted and negatively impacts your credit rating.

Look at all your revolving credit facilities and see how you can go about paying extra into each of these monthly. This, in itself, will help to improve your credit rating because it indicates that you can not only afford the debt that you have but that you can pay more than strictly necessary. It also helps to reduce the balance faster.

You would be amazed at how much faster your debt will reduce when you start paying more than the minimum monthly installment. Remember that the interest charged is calculated on the daily balance used so everything you do to reduce that balance is helping you – even if it means paying an extra ten dollars a month.

Pay Down Your Debt

You knew that this one was coming – it is advice that we hear all the time. Nevertheless, it is really good advice. You need to start targeting specific accounts in order to either pay them off or to pay them right down.

As you are paying more than the monthly minimum on all your credit accounts, you can now separate the credit accounts into two basic categories – revolving credit and installment credit.

Remember how we discussed that revolving credit was a more open-ended agreement? It is best to keep only one or two of these accounts at most and to ensure that they are way within their limits. Start by targeting the account with the highest interest rate and pay as much extra money into it as possible on a monthly basis. When it is paid off, apply that payment to the account with the next highest interest rate until that is paid off and so on, until all your accounts are paid off.

Choose one or two credit cards and store cards with the best deals in terms of fees and interest and close all the rest down completely.

It is a good idea to close down inactive accounts because, even when inactive, they still do have an impact on your overall potential debt exposure. You also do not want to have to pay annual fees for absolutely nothing, or risk damaging your credit score because you have annual fees accruing and going unpaid when you did not know about them.

Manage Your Credit Limits

One useful trick, and one I advocate only if you have firm discipline is to accept credit limit increases on your remaining accounts, within reason. Whilst your overall credit exposure is a factor, maintaining your cards balances at no more than 30% of your limits has a much more positive impact on your credit rating.

You might find that as your credit rating improves, you are offered credit increases. If this will put you closer to only using 30% of your limit, and if it is NOT going to increase your spending, this can be a quick and easy way to improve your credit rating.

If, however, you are concerned that you may max these cards out in a moment of weakness, skip this step altogether.

Start Working the System

In this chapter, we will look at ways to proactively work the system so that you can improve your credit rating even further. There is a big disclaimer for this section, though – I am going to advise applying for credit – if you do not have the self-discipline to stop spending money unnecessarily (no judgement here, I used to spend money to make myself feel better) it is better to pay all your debt down and only keep one emergency card.

You Need Some Credit

I mentioned briefly that I had been where you are now – I too once had bad credit. That quite frankly is an understatement. At one stage, I excelled at living beyond my means. I would use one credit card to pay the next and was eventually in so much debt that I ended up having to move back home with my parents and having to sell my apartment at a loss to prevent foreclosure. I also had my car repossessed. So, as you can see, my credit was destroyed!

As a result, when I started coming out from under it, I never wanted to see another credit card in my life again. I swore that if I couldn't afford to pay for anything cash, I would just go without it. This did work for some time but it did not help me to improve my credit score.

You see, although I had paid up all the arrears and gotten the negative listings removed, I was still considered a bad credit risk simply because I had no credit accounts at all. Now, how's that for irony – at first, I couldn't get credit because I had too much credit and then I couldn't get credit because I had no credit.

The problem with having no credit at all is that there is nothing that shows how well you can actually manage your debt. That is where the payment history comes back into play. When you have an active credit account and are paying it on time every month, you actually help to flesh out the picture of you as a responsible borrower.

Keep about two credit accounts so that you can show that you can manage your credit. You do need to keep them active, so do use them and make sure that they have a small balance on them. Do not max them out and pay them on time every month and your credit score will continue to rise.

Getting a Secured Credit Card

Of course, if you have no credit facilities because you were in a situation like mine, getting new facilities can be tough. What you can do is apply for a secured credit card. With a secured card, you will need to have money in some sort of savings account that can be offered as collateral against your spend on the card.

Your credit limit will match the funds that you have saved and you won't be allowed to exceed this but this can be a really great way to help to establish a credit history.

It is important to ensure that the card is actually a credit card and that you are not simply using the money in the savings so that you can ensure that you build your credit history.

Again, the normal rules apply – do not max out the card, always pay more than the minimum installment and make sure that the payments go through on time each and every month.

After you have established a good payment history – usually after about six months or so, enquire about switching to an unsecured credit card. Whilst a secured card does help to establish some payment history, it is not a true reflection of how you would handle a "real" credit limit and the information on the credit bureau would reflect that.

Get Installment Finance

Just like getting the credit card, having one installment credit facility on your profile helps to improve your overall credit rating and shows creditors that you are able to handle more than one type of finance.

Here again, though, you do need to let common sense prevail. If you have an existing loan, you do not need a second one. And do look for favorable rates and a good reason to get the money. "Improving my credit rating" is not a good excuse to borrow $20 000, for example. A small loan is all that is needed here so don't go applying for money for that overseas trip, etc.

The big advantage here is that the rates tend to be better because there is a set installment and you know that your debt will decrease each month. Not being able to draw down on the loan is one of the biggest benefits of installment finance versus credit card finance – at least you know that you will pay it off eventually.

Again, if you concerned that you will not be able to handle the payments, it is better to skip this step altogether.

Limit Credit Applications

Overall, it is best to limit the number of credit applications that you make. It is better to shop around for a good rate and apply at only one service provider than to apply at several. The reason for this is that every time you apply for a loan, an enquiry is made on your credit profile and potential creditors can view these enquiries as well.

Your credit score also does a bit of a hit when there are multiple enquiries over a short period of time. Think about for a second – if your friend was applying for money all over the place, would you think that they were desperate or would you think that they were credit worthy?

Don't apply for credit cards, store cards or loans unless you really need to and you can minimize the impact on your credit rating.

Be Consistent and Persevere

I wish I could tell you that if you did all these steps for a week, your credit rating would magically improve. Unfortunately, the system is not designed to work that way. Whilst there are things that you can do to improve your score, your past behavior will always play a role in your current credit score.

If you follow the tips in this book, you can expect to start seeing improvements in around about three to six months and the effects are cumulative as long as you are consistent in your efforts. Even if there is the odd setback, the cumulative efforts will soon start to bear fruit.

And just remember, the last six months are always given the most importance when it comes to determining your FICO score. Those looking over your credit report will also be more willing to give you a bit of leeway if they can see that you have made a real determined effort to improve the management of your financial affairs.

The benefits of being financially responsible are really worth the work – not only will you be able to save money on interest and insurance premiums but you might be in better standing to get the job of your dreams as well. And, best of all, you will have some peace of mind as well.

The Last Step

You will need to monitor your credit report to ensure that everything is on track. Take advantage of the free annual credit report to do a bit of a financial audit as well if your rating has improved. Call your insurance broker and have your policy reviewed. Do the same with your credit accounts as well – you might just manage to save some money on interest payments.

Make the steps that I have described in this book a habit – make it a priority to always pay your bills on time, never max out your cards, always pay a bit more than you have to and you will soon find that are once again in full control of your finances.

Conclusion

Well, here we are at the end of the book. I really hope that you enjoyed reading it and that you learned a lot that you can apply in your own life.

Remember that your credit score is always evolving so if you are battling with bad credit at this moment in time, it is not the end of the world. I know from personal experience how hard it can be to work at repairing your credit – especially after spending years having fun and getting it into a mess – but I also know how satisfying it is to restore your good credit rating.

Take the first steps in your journey to great credit today and who knows, maybe one day you have a score of 750 or higher!

Good financial management does not require that you are a financial guru or expert – all you need to do is to adopt the tips in this book and make them habits and you are all set.

Finally, could I ask you to do one thing for me? Would you take the time to leave a review and some feedback about my book on Amazon.com? I really would appreciate it.

All the best for your financial future!

Win a free

kindle
OASIS

Let us know what you thought of this book to enter the sweepstake at:

http://booksfor.review/rebuildcredit

www.ingramcontent.com/pod-product-compliance
Lightning Source LLC
Chambersburg PA
CBHW020958180526
45163CB00006B/2420